Jenny Wren
The Special Thank You

Shirley Kopp

A True Story

Written and Illustrated by Shirley A. Kopp

Dream Write Publishing Ltd.
P. O. Box 57083 RPO Eastgate
Sherwood Park AB T8A 5L7 Canada

www.dreamwritepublishing.ca

Jenny Wren
The Special Thank you

ISBN # 978-1-988723-87-7
Illustrations and Cover Art by Shirley A. Kopp
Cover and Book Design by Dream Write Publishing

Library and Archives Canada Cataloguing in Publication:

Jenny Wren - The Special Thank You
Kopp, Shirley A. (b.-) Edmonton AB

Available Print-on-Demand | Amazon

Dedication

To my Mother - Dorothy Christina Kopp
who first nurtured my love of nature.

To my best friend – Sharon Darlene Bunnin
who always believed in me, no matter what.

A Thank You to Helen Dodds
whose phone call began what turned out to be a beautiful story.

And a very special Thank You to Helen Lochr
who encouraged me, helped me edit,
and has always been right there with guidance and support.

I first saw them on the fence, small and dusky brown with a paler underside. With their short, rounded, lightly barred wings and upturned tails I knew they were 'House Wrens'.

I heard them in the nearby woods long before I saw them. Their singing exuberant – gurgling, bubbling, a series of trills and whistles rising and falling in a wrens' own beautifully orchestrated warble.

This was the song I first heard in my childhood; one I never tired of. My mother had given me my appreciation of nature at an early age. We especially loved the songbirds, the individual colours of each species and their unique calls. Mom taught me not to bother them when they were building their nests and raising their young, but to appreciate them from a distance. She referred to 'House Wrens' as 'Jenny Wrens'.

I am thrilled to see the male chose the little birdhouse I so carefully crafted and attached near the back of the yard beside a fence post.

When his mate agreed they began to build their nest in earnest. It takes many, many trips but they are set on their task. From the deck I watched while he started bringing twigs and grasses. It is a delight to watch him twisting and turning his little body into different positions, as he moves a twig so efficiently from his beak through the little hole. Sometimes he will toss out one twig only to go and find another more suitable one.

Contained within the twigs, the female constructs the cup of the nest with materials such as grasses, feathers, and other soft items.

A twig is often placed between the nest and the hole to protect the babies from intruders.

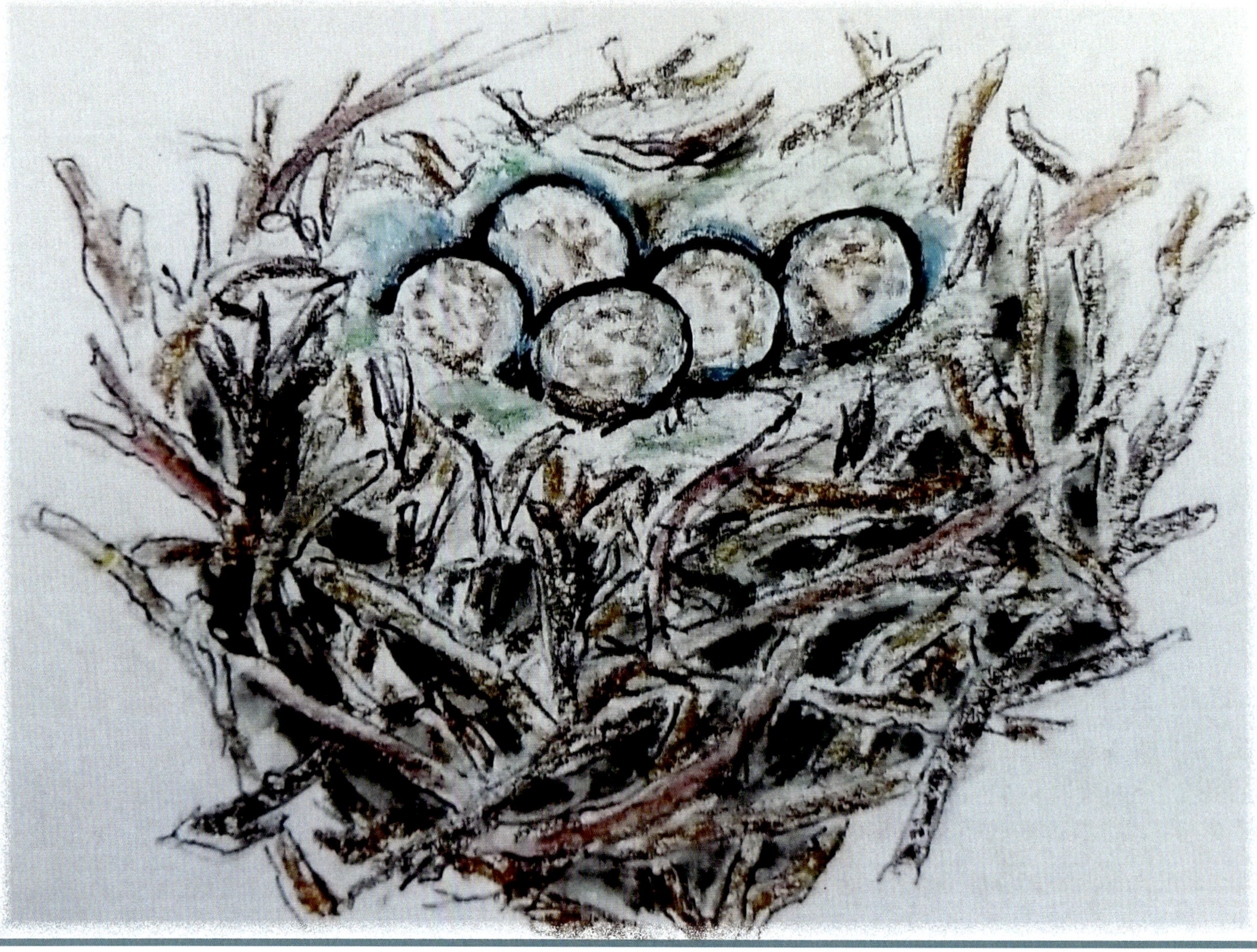

Once complete, I learn the female lays usually between 5 – 8 white eggs with brown speckles, which hatch in 12 – 13 days. They often raise more than one set of babies per year.

When the eggs hatch, both parents take responsibility for feeding them a diet of mostly insects and spiders.
Once fledged, I will feel sad to see them go.

During these times I only venture near when I need to weed the flower and shrub beds below. Then I would talk softly to them.

"It's okay, I'll be done soon. I promise I won't hurt you."

However, I am always warned away with their scolding chatter.

One particular afternoon, on a warm and radiant day, the sky a perfect cerulean blue with a dusting of cottony clouds and the sun the colour of bright yellow sunflowers, the phone rang.

I answered, "Hello," only to hear the anxious voice of my next-door neighbour, Helen.

"Shirley," she said. "Can you come right over? A bird flew in through the open door and I don't know how to get it out!"

Unsure of what I needed to do, I said, "Oh, my gosh, Helen. I'll be right over." My first thought as I hurried over was that I would assess the situation; then make a plan.

Apparently, the bird flew through the whole house and was now in the master bedroom. As I followed Helen in I could see the bird at the very top of the pole lamp near the ceiling in the corner of the room. I recognized immediately it was possibly one of my Jenny wrens. I knew the bird had likely flown in, got confused, and was unable to find its way out. I also knew that wild birds have a tendency to fly near the ceiling and don't realize they need to fly lower. I decided we needed to contain it, so as not to scare the little bird any further.

"Helen," I said calmly, "Would you please close the bedroom door and also the ensuite bathroom door since birds can injure themselves on mirrors?" Helen quietly did as I asked. Now contained, while the tiny bird stayed up high, I again asked Helen, "Would you please open the window and take out the screen?"

"Yes," she said, as she pulled back the curtain,
opened the window,
and removed the screen.

Not being able to reach the bird, I said, "Now, Helen, we need something to reach her with." While I kept an eye on Jenny, Helen slipped out and was able to find a thin green pole with a hard loop on the end about the size of a silver dollar.

"Perfect, Helen, thank you," I said upon her return. Next, I needed to gain the trust of my tiny friend, so I asked Helen to stay back and not move. I already began to talk softly and calmly to Jenny, so I continued.

"It's okay, I'm going to help you get out of here. You just need to trust me." This I repeated over and over in a soft tone so as not to scare her further. At the same time, I slowly raised the pole until the little loop was near her feet. I could see her watching my every move, still unsure. Over and over and over again, I repeated gently, "Come on, you can trust me. I promise I will get you out of here."

Eventually one tentative little foot came out and grasped the loop.

As I patiently waited, filled with hope now, but my arm getting very tired, I continued talking softly, and her other foot stepped on. I was thrilled but I also realized we had a long way to go to get to the open window. With the pole still held high, I continued.

"Hang on, stay with me, we can do this!"

I slowly made my way around the perimeter of the bed while glancing at where we needed to go. I continuously watched her as she kept tensing her tiny body, still obviously afraid and considering flight. "It's okay, you can trust me, we can do this," I repeated. It took what seemed a long time to reach the window, but when we did I gently lowered the pole at an angle toward the window until Jenny was below the frame.

Once there she felt the outside air and in a split second flew outside.

"Whew!" I let out a deep breath.
"That was tough."

Helen and I were ecstatic to know Jenny was out and safe. She called me 'The Bird Whisperer', but my joy was seeing Jenny back outside and feeding her babies once again.

A couple of days later, I was working my way down the flower and shrub bed busily pulling weeds, when I found myself near the birdhouse. While rising slowly, I said softly,

"So, how are you doing today, my little friends?"

Original 8 x 10 painting by Shirley Kopp

However, this time, instead of getting my usual scolding that precious little wren flew up on the fence, looked right at me, and sang to me. I was thrilled and voiced a heartfelt, "Thank You."

Whether it was the sound of my voice that helped Jenny Wren to trust me that day in Helen's house I will never know, but I was never scolded again for being too close. What I do know is – it was the most beautiful 'Thank You' I have ever received and one I shall never forget.

Things to be learned from this story:

BE OBSERVANT

There are a lot of wonders in our world if we take the time to notice. Many are at no cost, can be small, and completely unexpected.

BE RESPECTFUL

We all deserve our own space, including animals and plants.

BE KIND

Kindness is always the better choice. It will usually come back to you in return. It can change some thing's or someone's life.

BE PATIENT

Patience can give you a greater appreciation for what you can achieve, as well as unexpected rewards.
All animals, birds, and even people need the ability to do things in their own time – so allow that time.

BE GRATEFUL

Remember to say 'Thank you' whenever you are given help.

LOVE NATURE AND YOURSELF

Just like the birds, we are all unique.

By practicing all of the above your life can only be enhanced.

About the Author and Illustrator:
Shirley A. Kopp

Shirley grew up by Turtle Lake, Saskatchewan; now Kopps Kove. She went to school in Livelong and Turtleford, Saskatchewan.
Shirley received a General Art Certificate while taking a correspondence course from Art Inst. Schools, Minneapolis, Minnesota, during her High School years.

Shirley lived and worked in Edmonton, Alberta, in various capacities in the photographic industry. Shirley moved to Sherwood Park, Alberta, where she worked outdoors, part-time, for a condo corporation. She enjoys hobbies in art – mostly acrylic painting, being part of a writer's group, and various sporting activities. Shirley also does volunteer work in her community. This is Shirley's first book.

Manufactured by Amazon.ca
Acheson, AB

10669726R00017